A Matter of Survival

Ann Weil

Raintree

www.raintreepublishers.co.uk

Visit our website to find out more information about **Raintree** books.

To order:

☎ Phone 44 (0) 1865 888112

▤ Send a fax to 44 (0) 1865 314091

▤ Visit the Raintree bookshop at **www.raintreepublishers.co.uk** to browse our catalogue and order online.

First published in Great Britain by Raintree, Halley Court, Jordan Hill, Oxford OX2 8EJ, part of Harcourt Education. Raintree is a registered trademark of Harcourt Education Ltd.

Editorial: Lucy Thunder and Richard Woodham
Design: Michelle Lisseter, Carolyn Gibson, and Kamae Design
Picture Research: Melissa Allison
Production: Camilla Crask

Originated by Dot Gradations Ltd
Printed and bound in Italy by Printer Trento srl

ISBN 1 844 43843 0 (hardback)
10 09 08 07 06
10 9 8 7 6 5 4 3 2 1

ISBN 1 844 43858 9 (paperback)
11 10 09 08 07
10 9 8 7 6 5 4 3 2 1

British Library Cataloguing in Publication Data
Weil, Ann
A Matter of Survival: materials and their properties
530
A full catalogue record for this book is available from the British Library.

Acknowledgements
The publishers would like to thank the following for permission to reproduce photographs:
Alamy pp. 7 (Anthony Blake Photo Agency/Chris Seddon), 11 (Chris Prior), 29 (Classic Image); Corbis pp. 13 (Stuart Westmorland), 14–15 (Corbis); Getty Images pp. 5 (The Image Bank), 6 (Stockbyte), 14 (The Image Bank/Hans Neleman), 19 (Taxi), 22 (Taxi/David Nardini), 26–27(Photographer's Choice/Peter Hendrie); Harcourt Education pp. 7 (Tudor Photography with thanks to Beans of Bicester, UK), 16 (Tudor Photography), 20 left (Tudor Photography), 20 right (Mica Brancic), 21 (Tudor Photography); NHPA p. 24–25 (Christophe Ratier); Still Pictures p. 8 (Peter Schickert).

Cover image of a bottle in water reproduced courtesy of Getty Images (Taxi/David Nardini).

The publishers would like to thank Nancy Harris and Harold Pratt for their assistance in the preparation of this book.

Every effort has been made to contact copyright holders of any material reproduced in this book. Any omissions will be rectified in subsequent printings if notice is given to the publishers.

The paper used to print this book comes from sustainable resources.

Contents

Some words are printed in bold, **like this**. You can find out what they mean on page 30. You can also look in the box at the bottom of the page where they first appear.

Lost!

"This is your captain speaking. We have a problem. We are over the ocean. We need to land on water. Put on your life jackets. Repeat, put on your life jackets…"

You open your eyes. You are in the water. There is no sign of the plane. You are wearing a life jacket, but it isn't keeping you afloat. Should you take it off? It's a life-or-death decision.

Knowing about **materials** can help you decide. Everything is made of materials. The planets are made of materials. The ocean is made of materials. Even the air is made of materials. Different kinds of materials have different **properties**. A property is a way to describe or measure a material. One property of ocean water is that it is salty.

A matter of fact

*The pages of this book are made of paper. Paper is a material. The pages of the book are **flexible**. They can bend without breaking. Being flexible is a property of paper.*

flexible   able to bend without breaking
material   anything that takes up space
property   way to describe or measure a material

Floating away

A life jacket needs to be full of air to float. Air is a **gas**. The ocean is a **liquid**. A gas always rises to the surface of a liquid. This is because a gas has a lower **density** than a liquid. Density is how much of a **material** there is in a certain space. Density is a **property**.

You blow air into your life jacket. Now the life jacket is full of air. The air in the life jacket makes you float. You spot a small island in the distance and swim towards it.

Gases

A gas is a kind of material that can change size and shape. Balloons are filled with gas. The gas helps them float in the air.

A life jacket will ▶ only float if air is blown into it.

density   how heavy something is for its size
gas   type of material that can change size and shape
liquid   type of material that takes the shape of its container

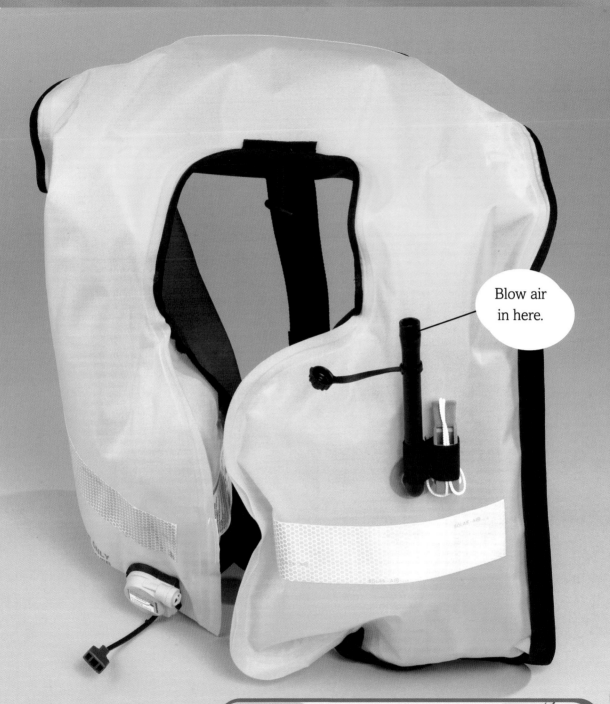

Blow air in here.

Liquids

A liquid is a kind of material that takes the shape of its container. Water is a liquid. When you pour water into a glass, it takes the shape of the glass.

Take shelter

You swim to the sandy beach. The island is beautiful. You are too tired to explore. You need to rest after your long swim. The sun is hot. You find shade under a coconut tree.

THUD! A falling coconut just misses your head. Coconuts are very hard. Hardness is a **property**. You don't want to be hit on the head by a very hard **material**. Resting under a coconut tree is a bad idea!

You pick some leaves from the trees. Leaves have two important properties. They are soft and **flexible**. Leaves can bend without breaking. You use the leaves to make a mat to sleep on. But it's too hot to lie out in the sun. You decide to build a shelter.

Material	Properties
coconut	hard
leaves	soft, flexible, light

◀ *Sand, water, leaves, and coconuts are all types of materials. They all have different properties.*

Under cover

The **properties** of wood make it good for building a shelter. Branches are the right shape for making a frame for the shelter. They are also light enough to move easily.

You push the ends of the branches into the sand. But they fall over! You need something heavy to hold the branches in place.

Rocks are heavy. They have a large **mass**. Mass is the amount of **material** something contains. There is more mass in a heavy rock than in a leaf, even if they are the same size.

You use the heavy rocks to hold the wooden frame in place. Now you need a roof to shade you from the sun. Leaves are light and **flexible**. They can bend without breaking. You weave some palm leaves together to make the roof. Now you have a simple shelter.

Material	Properties
coconut	hard
leaves	soft, flexible, light
branches	light, good shape
rocks	heavy, hard

mass   amount of material contained in an object

▼ *Branches and leaves are types of materials. They have properties that are good for building this shelter.*

11

Salty water

You are thirsty. You try drinking water from the ocean but it tastes salty. You cannot see the salt in the water. The salt has **dissolved** in it. If something dissolves, it spreads throughout a **liquid**. A liquid with something dissolved in it is called a **solution**. Ocean water is a solution. Salt is dissolved in the water.

Materials such as sugar and salt dissolve in water. Some materials do not dissolve in water. Plastic does not dissolve in water.

Material	Properties
coconut	hard
leaves	soft, flexible, light
branches	light, good shape
rocks	heavy, hard
ocean water	clear, salty

This water looks ▶ refreshing. But it is too salty to drink.

dissolve spread throughout a liquid
solution mixture where solids are evenly mixed in a liquid

Cracking coconuts

You don't drink the ocean water because it is salty. You
know there is **liquid** inside a coconut. You decide to crack
open a coconut. But the outside of the coconut is a **solid**.
A solid is a kind of **material** that takes up space and has
its own shape. The solid part of a coconut is very hard.
You need to find something very hard to open the coconut.
Knowing about **properties** can help you.

solid   type of material that has a fixed shape

You find a big rock further up the beach. You use the rock to crack open the coconut. Then you drink the delicious liquid inside.

You crack open more coconuts. You drink until you stop feeling thirsty. You also eat the insides of the coconuts. After eating the coconuts you explore the island.

Hardness

Hardness is a property. Diamonds are the hardest objects found in nature.

Survival box

You climb to the top of a hill to get a good view. The island is smaller than you thought. You can see all of it from where you are standing. There are no houses. There are no people. You are all alone. There is no one to help you. Your knowledge of science is now more important than ever.

You walk back to the beach. Your shelter has blown over in the wind! You're too tired to fix it. You wish you were home. You walk to the edge of the water and let the waves wash over your feet. What's that? A box has washed up on the beach! It must be from the plane. You open it and find these things inside:

- waterproof matches
- knife
- rope
- cereal bars
- chocolate
- bottled water
- pencil
- paper.

Changing materials

You drink the water and eat all the cereal bars. Then you watch the sunset. It is beautiful.

You will need a fire to stay warm at night. You can use the outsides of the coconuts as **fuel**. Fuel is anything that is burned to make heat or power. You use the matches to start the fire. The outsides of the coconuts quickly catch fire. The fire releases **energy**. Energy causes a change to happen. The energy of the fire makes you feel warmer.

The fire changes the wood to ashes. This is an **irreversible change**. An irreversible change makes one type of material become another. The new material has different properties from the old material. Ashes have different **properties** from wood. Irreversible changes usually cannot be undone. The ashes cannot be turned back into wood.

When fire turns wood to ▶ ashes, an irreversible change takes place.

energy	ability to make a change happen
fuel	anything that is burned to make heat or power
irreversible change	when a material changes into a material with

More changes

There is some rope and a knife in the survival box. You use the knife to cut the rope into smaller pieces. You use the pieces of rope to make your shelter stronger.

Small pieces of rope have the same **properties** as large pieces of rope. For example, small pieces of rope can bend like large pieces.

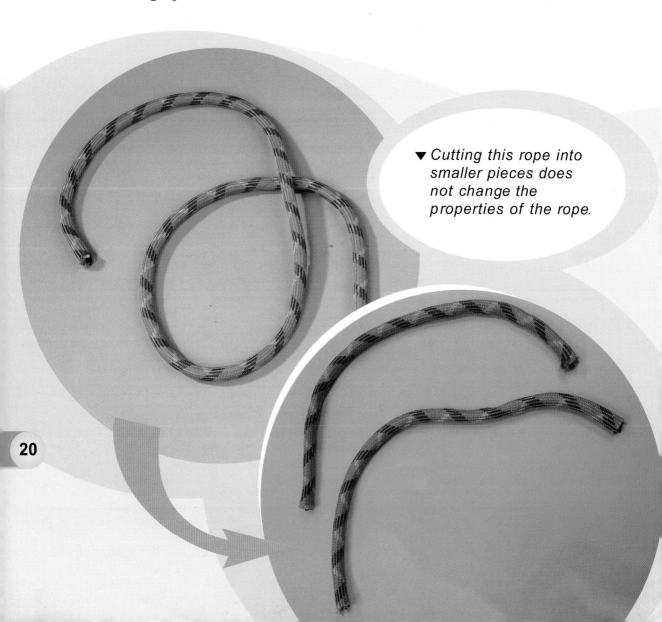

▼ Cutting this rope into smaller pieces does not change the properties of the rope.

You are very hungry. There is chocolate in the survival box. You unwrap the bar of chocolate. But it has melted in the hot sun! The chocolate has changed from a **solid** to a **liquid**.

Some changes can be undone. These are called **reversible changes**. No new **materials** are made in reversible changes. The melted chocolate will change back to solid chocolate if kept in a colder place.

▲ Chocolate is only a solid if it is kept at a low (cooler) temperature.

reversible change   change that can be undone

Message in a bottle

You find an empty bottle on the beach. The bottle has a cork. You write a note. Then you put the note inside the empty bottle. You put the cork on the bottle. This traps air inside the bottle. You throw it in the ocean and watch it float away. You hope that someone will find it.

Branches and seaweed are also floating in the water. These things are **buoyant**. Buoyant things float on top of water.

Material	Property
coconut	hard, buoyant
leaves	soft, flexible, light, buoyant
branches	light, good shape, buoyant
rocks	heavy, hard, not buoyant
seaweed	buoyant
air	buoyant

◀ *This bottle is buoyant.
It floats in water.*

buoyant   able to float in a liquid or gas

Storm warning

You hear a sound. Is it a plane? No, it's thunder! It starts to rain. Water fills the empty coconut shells. You drink some of the water from the shells. Then you crawl under your shelter and fall asleep. When you wake up, the sun is shining. The coconut shells are empty! What happened to the water?

The water **evaporated**. When a **liquid** evaporates it changes from a liquid to a **gas**. The heat of the sunlight changed the water to a gas. Water as a gas has a greater **volume**. Volume is the amount of space taken up by something. The gas takes up more space than the water did.

These storm clouds ▶ will bring fresh water to drink.

evaporate   when a liquid turns into a gas
volume   amount of space that something takes up

Rescued!

The rain put out your fire. You try to start a new one, but everything is too wet. You use up all the matches but you still can't make a fire.

You hear something. Is it more thunder? No, it's a plane! A seaplane lands on the water near the beach. The pilot steps out. You're rescued!

The pilot helps you into the plane. She gives you a cold drink. You start to tell her how you survived. "It was easy," you say, "because I knew about **properties**. I knew that rocks are heavy and hard. I knew that –"

VRROOOOM! The sound of the plane's engine drowns out your voice. You sit back and relax. There will be plenty of time to talk about your adventure when you get home.

Castaway survivor

A sailor called Alexander Selkirk was left alone on an island for four years. This happened around the year 1700.

He used branches, grasses, and goatskins to build a shelter. He chose these **materials** because of their **properties**. The grasses were **flexible**, for example. They could bend around the shelter and make a roof.

He also made tools. He found metal that washed up on the beach. He used hard rocks to beat the metal and make tools.

Selkirk was alone for so long that he forgot how to speak. At first his rescuers did not understand him. Selkirk's amazing story interested many people. Daniel Defoe wrote *Robinson Crusoe* based on the real-life adventures of Alexander Selkirk.

This picture shows Alexander ▶ Selkirk being rescued. He had lived alone on the desert island for four years.

Glossary

buoyant able to float in a liquid or gas. A life jacket is buoyant because it floats in water.

density how heavy something is for its size. A gas has a lower density than a liquid.

dissolve spread throughout a liquid. Salt and sugar will dissolve in water.

energy ability to make a change happen. When fire burns it releases energy.

evaporate when a liquid turns into a gas. Puddles dry up because the water evaporates.

flexible able to bend without breaking. Leaves are flexible.

fuel anything that is burned to make heat or power. Wood, coal, and oil are types of fuel.

gas type of material that can change size and shape. The air around us is a gas.

irreversible change when a material changes into a material with different properties. Irreversible changes cannot be undone.

liquid type of material that takes the shape of its container. Water is a liquid.

mass amount of material contained in an object

material anything that takes up space. Everything around us is made of materials.

property way to describe or measure a material. A property of this page is that it can bend.

reversible change change that can be undone. Melting chocolate is a reversible change because the chocolate will become solid again if it is cooled down.

solid type of material that has a fixed shape. This book is a solid.

solution mixture where the solids are evenly mixed in a liquid. Sea water is a solution because salt is dissolved in it.

volume amount of space that something takes up.

Want to know more?

Books

- *Hatchet*, Gary Paulsen (Macmillan, 2005)
- *Island of the Blue Dolphins*, S. O'Dell (Longman, 1999)
- *Materials and their Properties*, Angela Royston (Heinemann Library, 2003)
- *Robinson Crusoe*, Daniel Defoe (Abdo, 2002)
- *Swiss Family Robinson*, Johann Wyss (Wordsworth, 1993)

Movies and DVDs

- *Swiss Family Robinson* (1960) is the film version of the book by Johann Wyss.

Websites

- Zoom into a tin can, and try crushing concrete at:
  www.strangematterexhibit.com
- Learn about the properties of all sorts of materials at:
  www.bbc.co.uk/schools/revisewise/science/materials
- Get help with homework, and free clip-art, at:
  school.discovery.com/students/

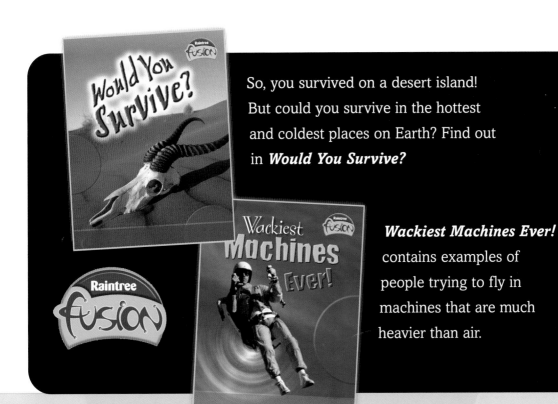

So, you survived on a desert island! But could you survive in the hottest and coldest places on Earth? Find out in **Would You Survive?**

Wackiest Machines Ever! contains examples of people trying to fly in machines that are much heavier than air.

Index